"Nevertheless"

Author Elder Bobby Morgan Sr.

Nevertheless
By: Elder Bobby Morgan Sr.
Designed: Isaac Brown III
Cover created: Jazzy Kitty Publishing
Logo designs: Andre M. Saunders and Leroy Grayson
Editor: September Summer
Co-Editor: Anelda Attaway

© 2017 Bobby Morgan Sr.
ISBN: 978-0-9988433-0-8

All rights reserved. This book is protected by the copyright laws of the United States of America. This book may not be copied or reprinted for commercial gain or profit. The use of short quotations or occasional page copying for personal or group study is permitted and encouraged. Permission will be granted upon request. Some actual scripture was used. For Worldwide Distribution, available in Paperback and eBook. Printed in the United States of America. Published by Jazzy Kitty Publishing, utilizing Microsoft Publishing Software.

ACKNOWLEDGMENTS

First, I thank God for my gift of writing.

To Mattie Brown and Robert Morgan Sr., thank you for my parentage and introducing me to the Lord. I Love You.

A special thank you to Sister Bobbie Dearion for her time and contribution to this book, and to her Pastor.

DEDICATIONS

This book is dedicated to those who believed in me and stayed true to the will and Word of God. *(Philippians 4:13) I can do all things through Christ that strengthens me.* Thank you for your support and love. Your kind words were encouraging and your prayers welcomed.

I would also like to dedicate this book to people like me. For people who have been broken many times in many different areas of their lives; and to those who felt like you were too deep in sin, and too filthy for God to pull you out and to use you for His glory. I further include those family members who have become victims of generational curses.

TABLE OF CONTENTS

INTRODUCTION..i

CHAPTER 1-Nevertheless..01

CHAPTER 2-Leadership..06

CHAPTER 3-Self-promotion..08

CHAPTER 4-The Joys of Life..10

CHAPTER 5-Forgiveness...12

CHAPTER 6-Surrender...14

ABOUT THE AUTHOR..19

INTRODUCTION

This is a book of information, encouragement, and leadership. It is a personal account of how submission and knowledge are power against the enemy. This book in chief part is how to press forward in spite of hardships and trials. It addresses how to recognize authority, and makes you aware of how operating in the Spirit of the Lord neutralizes the spirits of envy, rebellion, and anger. Submission through the Will of God is promoted. "Nevertheless", was inspired by personal accounts in my life which caused me to seek God's Word with a greater desire. This led me to the understanding that submission is a requirement for true Godly happiness.

CHAPTER 1

Nevertheless

"Nevertheless" is one of, if not, the highest form of submission. Submission can only exist when authority is present. The principle of "Nevertheless" isn't something that just happens; it's something we should strive to achieve. When Jesus was in the Garden of Gethsemane, He prayed to His Father Jehovah *(If it be possible, let this cup pass from me. Nevertheless, let not mine but thou (your) will be done.)* In one statement Jesus accomplished what mankind has struggled with for over 2000 years. From his own statement, He expressed that He saw or knew of something that He didn't want to endure. However, He submitted without anger or remorse.

To submit is to follow; knowing how to follow is a lesson that cannot be passed over if one truly wants to lead. In the beginning, God created man, and out of man God brought forth a woman. He said she would be a helpmeet or *(helpmate)*. Her duties were to help the man. There are several things that went wrong in the garden:

1. She was found to be in the presence of bad company, which means ungodly counsel.

2. She acted on her own accord.

3. An even bigger mistake was what the man did. He did nothing. Remembering that this was the beginning of humankind, he should have brought forth a suitable judgment and punishment for her, much like a judge would do today if we were to find ourselves in court. Instead, he did nothing.

4. The biggest mistake made in the garden was when Adam gave up his position of leadership and began to follow Eve, instead of leading her. Adam failed to submit to the Will of God. It was God's Will for a man to lead his helpmate, not be led by her. Not being able to submit is being unable to follow. There was no *"Nevertheless"*. If Adam had said, Eve, you are bone of my bone and flesh of my flesh and I love you with all my heart; nevertheless, I must uphold the command given to me by God;" then the fall of mankind wouldn't have happened.

Now, please understand the fall was in no way the woman's fault. No, she shouldn't have had the conversation; and yes, she was tricked. The Bible even refers to the woman as the weaker vessel, but the responsibility of leading was placed solely on the man. The Law of Physics states that two bodies cannot occupy the same space. There is a spiritual concept here, as well. The woman can seek to lead, but she can't truly do so unless the man steps down. The fall in the garden belonged to the man alone. When we operate on feeling, logic and emotion, we open the door to fear, envy and anger. Fear, envy and anger will almost always cause us to make a bad decision. To be in compliance with the Will of God, we must be Christians, which means to be Christ-like. He gave up His Will in order to achieve the will of the One who was greater.

There is a worldly concept that if I do my best, everything will be OK. The reality of this statement is that *"I" and "My,"* most of the time will not include God. One of the biggest problems with today's society is that we have too many ideas. Too many ideas make us incompatible or disables us from being led by God. The Bible says "Lean not to your own understanding." This statement signifies that our comprehension skills are limited. The Bible, the Word of God, doesn't leave us stranded. It says acknowledge Him in all things and He will direct thy path. This statement, once again, requires us to submit/follow. It asks us to take a look at our broken and battered lives, and to look in the faces of our needy children, our homeless, the drug addicted, etc., and say *"Nevertheless."* This would say to God, "My life is yours and I submit my will unto you. I will follow you wherever you go."

There are often times when we let our desires take the place of our needs. One of the highest divorce rates is that of Christian couples. God does not stop being God once we say, "I do." The work He has for you to do does not go away; one's calling is not removed just because we get married. If one is truly sold out to God, he/she will support and enhance their spouse's walk with Christ. However, when one seeks to please himself/herself or put his/her desire ahead of the needs of the God-ordained unit, the relationship will suffer. This is when we need a "Nevertheless" moment. This is the moment when someone says, "I choose love."

To love God is to walk by faith and not by sight. Faith is the substance of things hoped for, the evidence of things not seen. There is no other way with God, except the right way. The Bible says to do things decently and in order. Let's say that you and your spouse can't agree, you can't get the kids to listen, the car is broken down and your job is hanging by a thread. This is when emotion, logic and desire become the dominant force driving your decision making. Your judgment is clouded, the accusations begin to fly, your anger grows and the separation slowly grows.

For those of us who truly love God, we will revert back to "Nevertheless." We seek God's Word and guidance, which leads us back to the structure He has already given. This is a form of submission, and it makes a bold statement which is, "I'm ready to follow." The man is saying "I'll follow you, God;" and the woman is saying, "I'll follow you, man, as you follow God." This is the moment when most Christians realize that Jesus' statement of letting thou will be done, is submission that requires unwavering faith. Most relationships fail because there is a breakdown in command. God has given a clear path to follow and a structured chain of command. Even though it may seem hard, putting God first will always yield Godly results.

CHAPTER 2
Leadership

Leadership is something in which a lot of women have excelled. This is due in large part to men walking out on their responsibilities. God gave man the responsibility of being the head of the woman. This is a very important role, as it has been proven that wherever the head goes, the body will follow. When the leadership role is taken for granted, it opens the door for all sorts of demonic forces to come in. The leader is the shepherd, the protector, the provider, and, most of all, the teacher. Patience, kindness, compassion and strength are all lessons that the leader will teach, and they are all taught by the way he leads. It is for this reason that the leader must operate in the authority God has given.

Leadership is often lonely because your decisions will not always please those under you, and around you. Leadership requires the ability to put more focus on your vision while still dealing with present trials. This is something that most people don't understand, especially those close to you. Most people want what they want, and they want it when they want it. When the leader is not allowed to meet their needs inside of their time frame, some people lash out in anger. There will be every reason under the sun given to a leader to make him/her feel as if he or she is wrong; that they don't hear God; or that somebody else's idea is better than the leading of the Holy Spirit. This is when we need to embrace "Nevertheless." When all seems lost, one is willing to let go in order to please God and do what is right. Everything that goes wrong will be said to be your fault. The world will call you a fool for not seeing and thinking logically.

Job was asked by his friends what sin he committed to bring on such sickness. His wife told Him to curse God and die, but what Job said let us know that Job had a "Nevertheless" moment. His response was, "Though he slays me yet will I trust Him." His family and friends couldn't understand that Job's love for God would not allow him to take another path. His body was wracked with pain and his heart was broken in pieces, but his faith was intact. The Bible says without faith it's impossible to please God. The leader must lead by faith, even when it causes him to be an outcast in his own home. Leading in faith means walking in obedience, and obedience is better than sacrifice. The leader must embrace "Nevertheless," for this is what it means to be a Christian. You are to promote God's Will and not your own.

CHAPTER 3

Self-promotion

Self-promotion is one of the most common factors in causing people to be out of position. Self-promotion promotes one's will instead of God's. When Jesus walked among us, He was adamant about the fact that He had to be about His Father's business. His Father's will was always at the forefront. Self-promotion won't allow one to see or accept anyone's view but one's own. The problem with this is what one faces every day. That is, when a person does other than what's expected of him or her, self-promotion makes an individual be the center of attention.

There should only be one center in the life of any Christian, and that center should be Christ. Most disagreements, whether it be marital, sibling or friendships, are fueled by self-promotion. Arguments will happen, but can be ended quickly by remembering Jesus in the Garden. In that moment, He gave up all to gain even more. You may say what could be more than all? The Bible says, "We are more than conquerors..." This can only be achieved by giving up and giving into God. The disagreement will be dissolved not by who's right or wrong, but by the Word of God. By putting God first, one embraces "Nevertheless," and this neutralizes the spirit of self-promotion and restores God back to His rightful place as the leader and the head.

CHAPTER 4
The Joys of Life

The joy of life for a Christian is knowing that he/she is in a relationship with someone who will love him/her without fail. Many of us are satisfied with this because we know all is well in the universe. The sun rises and sets at the Word of our God.

Yet, there are others who are only happy when things are going their way. This is unhealthy because if it is done too much, one will lose his/her ability to see the bright side. For example, what is the bright side of a rebellious child? The bright side is that he/she is still alive and has not died in their sins. This means that he or she has a chance to repent. What is the bright side to a dirty home? One has to clean all day; it seems no one wants to help and no one gets paid. The bright side, is that you could be the man living under the bridge, or you could be the woman with child and no place to lay her head. A "Nevertheless" attitude says, "I thank God for whatever God has given me. Whatever I've suffered, it's OK, and whatever I've lost, it's OK.

The Bible says all good things come from above; and it also says all things work together for the good for those who love Christ and are called according to His purpose.

Nevertheless

The joys of life are not based on money, possessions, or a flawless routine. They are based on a relationship with Christ. There will be days when one will cry, and there will be days when you quite frankly want to give up But, be encouraged, dig deep and say, "Nevertheless," not my will but yours be done. Then, lay down and sleep a sound sleep because of the joy of knowing that if you die tonight your soul is right with the Lord and that can't be taken away. That is a peace that surpasses all understanding.

CHAPTER 5

Forgiveness

Forgiveness is something a lot of people struggle with and, quite frankly, don't understand.

Forgiveness is needed more by the one giving it, than the one receiving it. Forgiveness is a personal issue between one's self and God. Without love we don't give true forgiveness; we give temporary passes and operate with certain tolerances to achieve a desired outcome. But when God is in the picture, forgiveness is accompanied by freedom.

The Bible says whom the son sets free is free indeed. When God forgives you, He doesn't hold it over your head for later use. He does not use it as leverage to achieve a certain or desired outcome. He does it because he loves us. One must embrace and understand the importance of giving forgiveness in order to truly be thankful for being forgiven. If not, self-promotion is still at work and a personal agenda is still trying to be achieved.

Unforgiveness turns into bitterness, bitterness leads to rebellion and rebellion at its root is satanic because it stands in direct opposition to the Word and Will of God. This is why we must, as Christians, embrace "Nevertheless."

"Nevertheless" recognizes authority and subdues rebellion.

When we truly forgive, it is in spite of how we have been, or will be hurt. "Nevertheless" (Submission to God's Will) will oftentimes cause us to be in a storm longer than desired, in order for someone else to see the way out.

CHAPTER 6

Surrender

This is something that most of us will deny, but if we look deep, we will see that there is a surrender problem in the body of Christ. There is a clear order in biblical text, one not based on man or woman, but on the statutes given to us by God. We will never truly surrender until Christ is fully accepted. We take Him in part, holding on to what benefits us; but if we really surrender we would empty our knowledge and desires unto Him.

"Nevertheless" cannot be attained without surrender. Tears, blood, and time are part of our surrender. There will be times when one will sleep at work because he/she has cried all night. There will be times when a person will feel like he/she doesn't deserve to be looked at or even heard; based on what someone else says one's worth is. There will be times when you do your best and someone else decides that 'God made a mistake by putting you in the position you are in', and then proceed to tear your life into shambles.

To surrender at a time like this seems impossible, however, it's your only way out. The thief on the cross changed the course of his life in the final minutes of his life by surrendering. He had never seen Jesus work a miracle; and he had never been baptized. He had not led a Christian life and according to the world, he was getting what he deserved. It looked as if he had no hope and then he entered into "Nevertheless." He knew he was going to die. He knew there was not going to be an escape from his punishment, but he recognized Jesus for who He was and confessed anyway. Surrender + "Nevertheless" = Paradise.

As stated earlier, this book was inspired by personal accounts and trials in my life. In 2014, I suffered tragedies in my life that I never expected. My child from my first wife would basically be abandoned by her, and he of course would come to live with me. It was a joy and a blessing to have him, seeing that is what I wanted anyway. However, the heartbreak that he suffered seemed at times unbearable for us both.

Only seven months later, my oldest son's mother would be murdered. Even though my two older sons lived with me, they had begun to re-establish the relationship they once had with their mother. Her death would prove to be devastating.

Several months earlier, before all of these events began to unfold, my wife of almost 5 years decided she wasn't going to wear her wedding ring anymore because, in her words, "It didn't seem like a marriage." I was still Pastoring the church, encouraging the congregation, and going to work every day. I was still praying and believing God for a miracle, but I was torn up on the inside. My pain was eased by my children.

From a prior relationship, I had been blessed with my oldest child Lavincia, who I raised alone. Sierra and Makayla were children from my first wife, but God saw fit to allow me to raise them also.

From my second marriage, I would gain two sons, Gavin and Kieton; one biological and both, gifts from God. In my pain and struggle, God would use them to pull me from the edge of destruction. He showed me their needs and desires, and then let me know that I couldn't meet them. He also assured me that He could and would; but it would be done through me. So, if I gave up, they would suffer. Knowing that besides living for Him, there is no greater drive in me than my family; I picked myself up and did as Paul said, "I (began to) press toward the mark of the high calling which is in Christ Jesus."

When Satan came to me and told me that after all I had suffered, that I had a right to quit; God would intervene and remind me of how Christ suffered. Then, he told me to get a bottle of water and an aspirin and keep on going.

There were times when I was sick, there were times when the money got short and we were hungry. There were times when I hid out in my room because I didn't want my children to see me cry. I was looking for that gigantic blessing to come, so everybody could see it and know that I was a child of God. But, I keep getting the same message, "Look at what He suffered for you, and now keep going."

My messages at church changed, they became more encouraging. I was promoted on the job, the kids were doing better, but I was still hurting. Like any true Christian, I turned to my God for answers and guidance. Like I had been hearing for close to a year; the Spirit of the Lord would answer with "just keep going." God was teaching me the basics of "Nevertheless." He was teaching me how to suffer gracefully. The word of God says if you suffer with me you shall also reign with me. If you want to reign with God you have to know how to suffer.

"Nevertheless" is the foundational principle of suffering gracefully. It brings you face to face with submission and authority. One day, on my way home from work, I would meet a woman who would truly change my life. I understood in that instance why His message for so long was, "keep going." He knew where he had placed her; and He knew where he had positioned her.

He had told me all those months to keep going because He was directing me to the miracle I had been asking for. "Nevertheless" tested my faith. God needed to know that He could trust me with my blessing. Faith that hasn't been tested is faith that can't be trusted. When I thought the door before me led to my end, God showed me it was the door to a new beginning. Now, happily married to a woman whom God has chosen for me, we pray for your strength in your seasons of "Nevertheless."

ABOUT THE AUTHOR

Elder Bobby Morgan, Sr., Pastor of the East Side Christian Church, is the father of eight children. He was introduced to the Lord as a child, but it would be at the age of twenty-seven that he truly would accept the Lord. On September 26, 1997, Elder Morgan laid down his banner and took up the Blood-Stained Banner of the Lord. Three years later in 2000, he accepted his call into the ministry. After another three years, and being licensed and ordained, he preached his first sermon. After a hard-fought battle to keep his marriage, it ended in divorce.

Then God would reveal by way of the Holy Spirit, God's will for Elder's life; to preach, teach, write and pray for the salvation of humanity. While still pastoring, he started the U.C.F. (United Christian Fellowship), an organization which encompasses all denominations; and seeks to unify the body of Christ and to marry believers to the Will and Work of Christ.

www.ingramcontent.com/pod-product-compliance
Lightning Source LLC
Chambersburg PA
CBHW070554300426
44113CB00011B/1905